AUG 2 1 2018

THE OCEAN WORLD

A FINDING DORY DISCOVERY BOOK

By Paul Dichter

Special thanks to Ed Mastro, Exhibits Director
Cabrillo Marine Aquarium, San Pedro, CA

Lerner Publications • Minneapolis

Lerner Publications Company
A division of Lerner Publishing Group, Inc.
241 First Avenue North
Minneapolis, MN 55401 USA

For reading levels and more information, look up this title at www.lernerbooks.com.

Main body text set in Mikado.
Typeface provided by HVD Fonts.

Library of Congress Cataloging-in-Publication Data

The Cataloging-in-Publication Data for *The Ocean World: A* Finding Dory *Discovery Book*
    is on file at the Library of Congress.
ISBN 978-1-5415-3259-5 (lib. bdg.)
ISBN 978-1-5415-3272-4 (pbk.)
ISBN 978-1-5415-3263-2 (eb pdf)

Manufactured in the United States of America
1-44849-35719-1/16/2018

CONTENTS

The ocean is an amazing place. It is full of marvelous creatures . . . like Dory! Let's discover the ocean that Dory and her friends call home.

WELCOME TO THE OCEAN!

SO MUCH OCEAN!

More than 70 percent of our planet is ocean. The ocean is home to more than a million animals and plants. The water in rivers and lakes is fresh water. The water in the ocean is salty!

Arctic

Pacific

Atlantic

Pacific

Indian

Southern

OCEAN HABITATS

The ocean is a big place. Some parts of the ocean are warm. Some parts are cold. Ocean floors have mountains and valleys and even forests made of **kelp**! Different parts of the ocean are home to many different creatures.

BLUE TANG

Dory is a **blue tang**. Blue tangs are saltwater **fish** that live in **coral reefs** and rock-filled waters close to shore. Blue tangs can't survive in the cold. They usually stay in warm parts of the ocean.

Let's meet some of Dory's underwater friends! Look, there's Nemo, Destiny, and Mr. Ray . . . and is that Hank too?

WATER-BREATHING OCEAN ANIMALS

WHALE SHARK

Do you know that Destiny is a **whale shark**? Whale sharks live in the warmer oceans of the world. They live near the surface, but they are able to dive thousands of feet under the water.

OCTOPUS

Octopuses like Hank live in all the oceans of the world. There are over three hundred kinds of octopuses! Many of them live in shallow water. Octopuses have eight legs . . . and three hearts!

CLOWN FISH

Nemo is a **clown fish**. Clown fish live in coral reefs. There are twenty-eight kinds of clown fish! They grow to about 4 inches (10 cm) long.

RAY

Mr. Ray is a spotted eagle **ray**. Eagle rays live in warm, shallow water near the coast. Rays hunt for clams, crabs, **sea urchins**, octopuses, and squid on the ocean floor. Their eyes are on top of their heads.

Not all of Dory's friends are fish. (Just look at Hank!) Dory is friends with all kinds of animals. Some of them live under the water, and some live on the ocean's surface. Say hello to Bailey, Crush, and Squirt. Oh! Here are Fluke and Rudder too!

AIR-BREATHING OCEAN ANIMALS

BELUGA WHALE

Dory's friend Bailey is a **beluga whale**. Beluga whales live in the cold water of the Far North. Beluga whales are **mammals**, not fish. Fish breathe by taking oxygen out of the water, have cold blood, and many lay eggs. Mammals breathe air to get oxygen, have warm blood, and even have hair. Beluga whales usually swim just under the surface of the ocean. This way they can come up to the surface to breathe air whenever they need it!

SEA LION

Fluke and Rudder are California **sea lions**. California sea lions live along the coast of the Pacific Ocean. They are at home on land and in the water. They spend most of their days above water lying on rocks, but they are amazing swimmers. They can even sleep in the water!

SEA TURTLE

Squirt and his dad, Crush, are **sea turtles**. Sea turtles have been swimming in the oceans since the time of the dinosaurs! Sea turtles can be found all over the world. They come up to the surface to breathe. They can hold their breath underwater for hours at a time!

Dory and her friends have something in common. They all breathe oxygen. Fish like Dory and Nemo get oxygen from the water. Octopuses like Hank do too. Mammals like Fluke and Bailey get oxygen from the air. So do reptiles like Crush and Squirt. And so do we!

HOW DIFFERENT SEA CREATURES GET OXYGEN

GILLS

Fish have **gills** next to their mouths. Gills are what let fish breathe underwater. The fish takes in a mouthful of water and pushes the water out through its gills. As the water flows through the gills, the gills take oxygen from the water for the fish to breathe. Octopuses have gills too, even though they are not fish.

HOLD YOUR BREATH

Mammals such as whales and sea lions can hold their breath for a really long time. This is so they can dive for food without needing to come up for air. Sometimes Bailey or Fluke go on deep dives. They can even slow down their hearts so that the oxygen in their lungs lasts a lot longer.

BLOWHOLES

Whales like Bailey have **blowholes** on top of their heads. Blowholes are like whale nostrils. Beluga whales come to the surface to breathe out—and take in a breath of fresh air—through their blowholes. When a beluga is underwater, it keeps its blowhole closed so water cannot get in.

Some animals can live on the land AND in the water. We call these animals amphibious. Dory's friends Fluke and Rudder are both **amphibians**. So is Becky the **loon**!

AMPHIBIOUS ANIMALS

FLIPPING FLIPPERS

See those big back flippers? They flip forward and become little feet when sea lions are on land. This lets them walk on all fours! It is a great example of an amphibian **adaptation**. A sea lion's back flippers are useful on land and in the water!

SUPER SWIMMERS

California sea lions are incredible swimmers! They normally swim along at 11 miles (18 km) per hour but can swim in bursts of up to 25 miles (40 km) per hour. That's pretty fast for an animal that can weigh 860 pounds (390 kg)! They can dive almost 1,000 feet (300 m) under the water, holding their breath the whole time.

LOONS

Loons are also amphibious. They are birds that live on the water. Loons are fast swimmers and even faster fliers! They can hold their breath for a long time. This lets them dive in the water to catch fish.

Some mammals breathe air but spend their whole lives in the ocean, like Dory's friend Bailey the beluga whale! Let's meet some other ocean animals that are like Bailey. These are **warm-blooded** mammals that never set foot on land.

NON-AMPHIBIOUS ANIMALS

SPERM WHALE

Meet the **sperm whale**! Sperm whales have huge brains. Their brains weigh almost 20 pounds (9 kg)! Sperm whales have teeth. They use their teeth to eat squid, fish, and octopuses. They live all over the world. They usually live in groups called **pods**.

DOLPHIN

Dolphins are some of the smartest animals in the world! Like beluga whales, dolphins live in the ocean but must go to the surface to breathe air. Just like whales, dolphins have blowholes on top of their heads. Dolphins live in most of the world's oceans.

BLUE WHALE

The **blue whale** is the largest animal on the planet. That includes land animals! They can be as big as 100 feet (30 m) long and weigh 160 tons (145 t). Blue whales have two blowholes and no teeth. They live all over the world. Unlike beluga whales and dolphins, they usually live alone.

Not all animals spend their whole lives in the same place. Just ask Dory and Nemo! But some kinds of animals actually make long journeys every year. This is called **migration**. Nemo's teacher, Mr. Ray, knows all about migration. Let's learn about it!

MIGRATION

WHY DO ANIMALS MIGRATE?

There are a few reasons why some ocean animals migrate every year. The big reason is to find food. Some animals migrate to head for warmer waters. Some animals migrate when they are ready to have babies.

MIGRATION PATTERNS

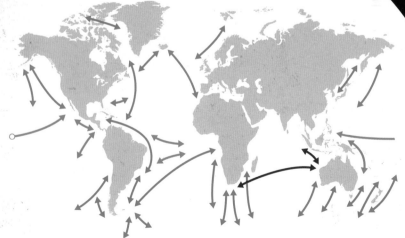

- GRAY WHALES, HUMPBACK WHALES, SOUTHERN RIGHT WHALES
- WHALE SHARK, GREAT WHITE SHARK
- LEATHERBACK TURTLES, GREEN TURTLES

WHALE MIGRATION

Beluga whales also migrate. Beluga whales live in the cold waters of the Far North. They travel south every fall to avoid the ice. They need to get to warmer waters before the northern waters start to freeze. One group travels more than 3,000 miles (4,800 km) . . . each way!

STINGRAY MIGRATION

A large group of stingrays is called a **fever**.

One type of ray is the stingray. A stingray migration is a magical sight. Twice a year, these normally solitary fish gather in huge groups and travel hundreds of miles! Why do they do this? We're not sure. We think it's probably to go to new feeding grounds.

Bailey is a beluga whale, and Destiny is a whale shark . . . so they must be the same kind of animal, right? Actually, they're very different! Whale sharks are fish. Beluga whales are whales, and whales are mammals. Let's discover some of the differences between fish and whales.

WHALES VS. FISH

ECHOLOCATION

Echolocation is a way that toothed whales like Bailey use sound to find and measure the shapes of things, just as we use our eyes. It helps whales get around! Here's how it works. Beluga whales make a clicking sound. That sound bounces off everything around them. Some clicks bounce back toward the whale, and the beluga listens for the echo. Whales can tell a lot about the environment from the sound!

BELUGA WHALE

BLUBBER

NO BLUBBER

FISH

BLUBBER

Under their skin, whales are covered from head to tail in **blubber**. Blubber is a thick layer of fat. It keeps whales warm in the cold ocean. Whales are warm-blooded mammals like us. They need the extra layer of fat to stay warm! So why don't fish have blubber? It's because fish are **cold-blooded**—their blood is the same temperature as the water around them.

THE TAIL FIN

Take a look at the tail **fins** of the whale shark and the beluga whale. Whale sharks, like all fish, have vertical tails. But whales have horizontal tails called **flukes**. That's because fish move their tails side to side, while whales move their tails up and down!

Let's find out how Dory and her friends move around. We call this **locomotion.** Have you noticed that Dory's friends come in many shapes and sizes? From Hank to Mr. Ray, each animal has its own way of getting where it's going!

LOCOMOTION

USE YOUR FINS!

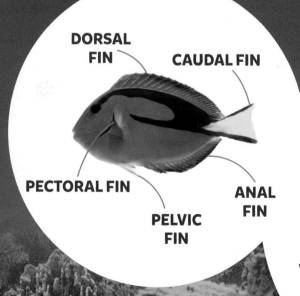

DORSAL FIN

CAUDAL FIN

PECTORAL FIN

PELVIC FIN

ANAL FIN

Fish like Dory use their fins to swim. Blue tangs have five sets of fins. Their dorsal, pelvic, and anal fins (on their backs and bellies) help them keep their balance in the water. Their caudal fins—on their tails—wave side to side and move them forward. And their pectoral fins—on their sides—help them make turns!

JET PROPULSION

Octopuses like Hank swim through the water headfirst. They take water in through their heads and squirt it out behind them. This pushes them forward really fast! But what about all those arms? Octopuses can also use them to crawl across the ocean floor.

WAVE IT AROUND

Rays swim by moving their whole bodies like a wave. Some of them also flap their sides (pectoral fins) like wings. This makes them look as if they are flying! One kind of ray, the roughtail stingray, can move really fast—up to 30 miles (48 km) per hour!

The ocean may be a dangerous place for some. Animals must stay safe to survive in the ocean. Let's look at a few ways Dory and her friends stay safe!

SURVIVAL IN THE OCEAN: STAYING SAFE

CAN'T REACH ME!

Blue tangs hide in small holes and cracks in coral reefs. When they're hiding, bigger fish like the yellowfin tuna or the tiger grouper can't reach them. Sometimes being small is a good thing! Many small fish live in coral reefs because there are so many good places to hide.

CAN'T CATCH ME!

Another way that small fish stay safe is by being fast! Sometimes the best defense is to swim away from danger. The bluelined wrasse fish is one of Dory's colorful neighbors on the coral reef. Even though they are tiny, they are some of the fastest fish in the ocean!

SAFETY IN NUMBERS

Many fish swim in large groups called **schools**. It's much safer swimming in a large group. Instead of seeing a tiny fish alone, hungry **predators** see a big mass moving through the water.

CAN'T SEE ME!

Many rays live on the ocean floor. They are amazing at hiding. Rays have different colored skin depending on where they live. This is so they can blend in with their surroundings. Some rays bury themselves under the sand to hide. When rays lie quietly in the sand, they can be almost impossible to spot! This lets them stay hidden from predators—and from prey!

Some of the same ways that ocean animals stay safe can also help them find food! Stingrays hide from both predators and prey. Schools of fish work together to stay safe and catch food. Let's learn about some of the special ways animals find and eat food!

SURVIVAL IN THE OCEAN: FINDING FOOD

FILTER FEEDERS

Big fish don't always eat big food. Just look at whale sharks! They are **filter feeders**. Whale sharks swim with their mouths open, sucking in lots of water filled with plankton, tiny fish, and krill. Then they filter the water through their gills and eat whatever is left!

ELECTRIC HUNTERS

Some rays eat other animals th...
the ocean floor. They have strong j...
can crush the shells of their prey. They don't use their eyes to find food. Instead, they use electricity! A ray has sensors near its mouth that can sense the electric charge of what it's hunting. Stingrays don't hunt with their stinging tail. Their tail helps protect them from predators.

SEA ANEMONE

The **sea anemone** may be pretty . . . but it's also dangerous for other small animals! Many think sea anemones look like flowers, but they are really animals. They spend their whole lives attached to something hard. Their tentacles have poison darts on them. They wave their tentacles around, waiting for a fish to swim too close. When a fish gets close, the sea anemone shoots out a poison dart from its tentacles, stunning the fish, and then it pulls the fish into its mouth.

Nemo and Marlin make their
But how can they live there a
by the anemone's stinging te
The answer might surprise you

MEET THE CLOWN FISH AND THE BLUE TANG

CLOWN FISH

Clown fish are covered in a
kind of slime that protects
them from the sea anemone.
There are only a few fish that
are safe from the poison darts
in an anemone's tentacles! Clown
fish make their homes in anemone
tentacles. The tentacles keep
clown fish safe from
predators.

HELP ME HELP YOU

Sea anemones catch their own food. The clown fish living between the tentacles eat the anemone's leftovers! Clown fish help sea anemones too! They do a wiggle dance by flapping their fins and swimming in circles. All that wiggling brings fresh water into the sea anemone. This helps the anemone grow big and strong!

BACK OFF, I'M A SURGEONFISH

Blue tangs like Dory come from a family of fish called **surgeonfish**. They get their name because they all have at least one sharp blade next to their tail. The blade is like a surgeon's knife! Blue tangs hide from predators in cracks in the coral. But they can also use their sharp blades to protect themselves when they are threatened.

Dory's friend Hank is a master of disguise. He is so good at hiding! Octopuses have many ways to stay safe. Let's learn more about octopuses.

MEET THE OCTOPUS

COLOR AND CAMOUFLAGE

Octopuses have tiny cells under their skin that can change color. They can make their skin match their surroundings. When they do this, they are almost impossible to see. Octopuses are so good at this that they can even make their skin look bumpy or spiky. This way, they match the rocks or coral they are lying on. Octopuses are some of the best hiders in the whole ocean!

HEY! NO GRABBING!

If a predator grabs an octopus's arm—the octopus can break off that arm and swim away. Later, once it's safe, the octopus will grow a new one. Good as new!

DON'T GET INKED!

One of the most amazing ways octopuses defend themselves is by squirting ink. Octopuses can release a cloud of dark ink to confuse their predators. While the predator is covered in ink, the octopus swims away . . . fast! The ink makes it hard to see. It also confuses a predator's sense of smell. Now that's how you hide!

Now you know that the ocean can be a scary place to live! We've seen a few examples of how Dory and her friends find food, stay warm, get oxygen, and stay safe. These are all ways that animals stay alive. Let's look at a few more ways animals can **camouflage** themselves in their environment.

CAMOUFLAGE

HIDING IN PLAIN SIGHT

Octopuses, stingrays, and **cuttlefish** are really good at blending in. They can be hard for predators or prey to see. But there's another way to stay safe, and that's to make sure you stick out! Some colors in the ocean mean danger. If an octopus suddenly starts flashing bright blue spots, it sends a message: stay away!

SHAPE-SHIFTER

Octopuses can change shape. They can squeeze into tiny hiding spots. The best shape-shifter is the mimic octopus. It tricks predators by mimicking a different animal—from a snake to a flatfish! It does this by changing shape and also changing color. It even changes the way it moves. It can pretend to be more than fifteen other animals!

MIMIC OCTOPUS

CUTTLEFISH
CAMOUFLAGE

Cuttlefish are also great at hiding. They can change color superfast! During the day, cuttlefish are bright and colorful. At night, everything changes. They can blend into the background in the blink of an eye. They can even change the texture of their skin!

The **open ocean** is made up of different zones. Each zone is at a different depth. And each zone has many different plants and animals. Many ocean animals spend their whole lives in the same zone. Some animals travel between zones. Dory has seen lots of different parts of the ocean on her adventures . . . but there are some places even Dory hasn't been! Let's explore.

OPEN OCEAN

OCEAN ZONES

SUNLIGHT ZONE
SEA LEVEL

SEA TURTLE

TWILIGHT ZONE
600 FEET (180 m)

SWORDFISH

MIDNIGHT ZONE
3,000 FEET (900 m)

ANGLERFISH

SWIMMING IN THE SUNLIGHT ZONE

Whale sharks like Destiny spend most of their time near the surface. This is the **sunlight zone**. Other animals that live in the sunlight zone are sea turtles, jellyfish, and seals. Whale sharks and their fishy friends travel far and wide. But there's a whole world deep underneath them that they never get to see!

ENTERING THE TWILIGHT ZONE

The deeper down we go, the darker it gets. That's because the light from the sun can't travel through all that ocean water. Once we get to 600 feet (180 m) below the ocean's surface, we enter the **twilight zone**. It's a lot colder in the twilight zone. There is no seaweed down here. Seaweed need sunlight! Squid, hatchetfish, and jellyfish live in the twilight zone.

DEEP IN THE MIDNIGHT ZONE

Once we get down to around 3,000 feet (900 m), we enter the **midnight zone**. Only very special animals live down here. It is freezing cold and pitch-black. The midnight zone is home to deep-sea worms and crabs. It is also home to a very interesting animal called the **anglerfish**. This funny-looking fish can make a small light above its head. It waves the light around to attract other fish to eat. Making light comes in handy in the midnight zone!

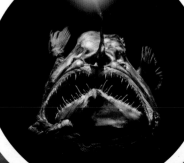

A lot of Dory's friends live close to the shore. **Coastal waters** are only a small part of the whole ocean. But more animals live in coastal waters than in the open ocean! The water near the coast tends to be warmer and shallower. Let's learn more about this **habitat**.

COASTAL WATERS

THE INTERTIDAL ZONE

Remember how we learned about the different zones of the open ocean? Well, coastal waters have zones too. There is a very busy place called the **intertidal zone**. The intertidal zone is where the land and the ocean meet! The sun's and the moon's gravity pull the ocean's water up and down the shore. The water is always moving. Snails, crabs, and mussels live in the intertidal zone.

SPRAY ZONE

SNAIL

HIGH TIDE ZONE

BARNACLES   SNAIL

MIDDLE TIDE ZONE

MUSSELS   CRAB

LOW TIDE ZONE

SEA STAR   KELP

SEA URCHIN

SEA OTTER

Sea otters are amphibious mammals, just like our friends Fluke and Rudder. That means they can live on both land and water. No wonder otters live in coastal waters! They breathe air just like sea lions. They can hold their breath for a few minutes when they dive for food. Sea otters don't have any blubber. Instead, they keep warm with the thickest fur of any animal in the world! Sea otters sleep floating on their backs.

SEA STAR

Sea stars can often be found in the intertidal zone. Sometimes sea stars are also called starfish, but they are not fish. They belong to a family of animals named **echinoderms**, or spiny-skinned animals. That family also includes sea cucumbers, sea urchins, and sand dollars. Sea stars live on the seafloor. They move very slowly, holding on in the strong surf with many tiny suction-cupped tube feet. Sea stars can regrow an arm if they lose one!

Let's learn more about the place Dory and Nemo call home: the **coral reef**! Coral is a tiny animal that lives its whole life in one place. Coral is a relative of the sea anemone. Coral reefs are like giant coral cities.

CORAL REEFS

CORAL IS COLORFUL

Coral reefs are found in the warmest ocean waters. They are busy places full of plant and animal life. They are also some of the most colorful places on Earth! The water in coral reefs is the clearest in the ocean. Water here is shallow and full of sunlight. Most animals that live on coral reefs have good eyesight. All those colors tell them what they might need to stay away from!

ANCIENT ALGAE

Algae are among the oldest living things on the planet! Algae are like sea plants. They cover coral reefs. There are many kinds of algae. Algae get their energy from the sun and make oxygen. Much of the oxygen on our entire planet was made by algae. Blue tangs like Dory eat algae. This is good for the coral reefs, because it keeps the algae from growing too fast and hurting the coral.

THE GREAT BARRIER REEF

The **Great Barrier Reef** is the largest coral reef in the world. It is off the coast of Australia. At 1,600 miles (2,600 km) long, it is the biggest living structure on Earth. It's so big you can see it from space. It's home to fish like blue tang and clown fish. Sea turtles, stingrays, sea horses, and hundreds of other animals also live there!

Another amazing ocean habitat is the **kelp forest**. These forests are made up of kelp, which is a kind of algae. They are just like forests on land, except with kelp instead of trees. Kelp forests grow in much colder water than coral reefs. Let's learn more about kelp forests!

KELP FORESTS

GROWTH SPURT!

Unlike coral, which grows very slowly, kelp is one of the fastest-growing life-forms on the planet! Giant kelp can grow up to 2 feet (0.6 m) in a single day! Kelp forests often grow in rough and choppy water. This is actually good for the kelp! The water is constantly moving. This keeps the water full of fresh nutrients that help keep the kelp fed and healthy. But if the surf is too rough, it might rip the kelp off the rocks.

SAFETY FIRST

Many animals rely on kelp forests for shelter. Just like coral reefs, the forests make great places to hide. Kelp forests can also protect animals from big storms! The thick kelp forests break up the energy from the huge waves. This keeps the ocean water from getting too rough for the animals.

OTTERS AND URCHINS

Many sea urchins live in kelp forests. Sea urchins are close relatives of the sea star! They also eat a lot of kelp. If there are too many sea urchins in a kelp forest, they will eat too much kelp and kill the forest! That's where sea otters come in. Many sea otters also live in kelp forests. And otters eat a lot of urchins! Otters help the kelp survive by keeping the sea urchin population under control.

We've learned about some of the ocean's many habitats. We've explored the dark, cold midnight zone. We've been to the sunny, warm coral reefs. These places are very important for the animals that live there. But the animals are important too! Let's learn more about how Dory and her friends are important to their habitats.

EVERYONE
PLAYS A PART

ECOSYSTEMS

An **ecosystem** includes all the plants and animals that live there. A habitat is the place where the animals and plants live. Each part of the ecosystem relies on the other parts to survive! We've seen a few examples of ecosystems. Blue tangs like Dory use coral reefs to find food and shelter. The coral reef helps the blue tang. The blue tang eats algae. This helps keep the coral healthy. That's a perfect example of a balanced ecosystem!

THE FOOD WEB

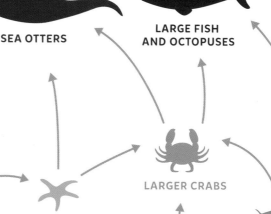

SEA OTTERS

LARGE FISH AND OCTOPUSES

SEA URCHINS

SEA STARS

LARGER CRABS

SMALL FISH

PLANKTON

KELP

A **food web** is a map of all the different plants and animals and what they eat. Each ecosystem has its own food web. Remember the sea otters and the sea urchins in the kelp forest? They are both part of the kelp forest's food web. Every single animal and plant in a habitat plays its part. Sometimes they eat food, and sometimes they are food!

PEOPLE AND THE OCEAN

People are part of the giant ecosystem that is the planet Earth! The ocean is very important to our survival. We are important to the ocean too. It is up to us to help keep this ecosystem balanced. We can do this by protecting ocean animals from overfishing and pollution.

We've learned so much about the ocean! We've met lots of Dory's friends and learned a lot about them. We know how they breathe and get around. We know how they protect themselves from danger. And we know about where they live. Let's say goodbye to Dory and her friends . . . for now!

GOODBYE FOR NOW!

GOODBYE FROM THE WATER BREATHERS!

Dory had so much fun exploring the ocean with you! So did Nemo, Marlin, Hank, Destiny, and Mr. Ray. By now you know a lot about clown fish, octopuses, whale sharks, rays, and blue tangs! They all swim differently. They all live in different parts of the ocean. One thing they have in common is they all breathe oxygen in water using their gills.

GOODBYE FROM THE AIR BREATHERS!

Bailey, Fluke, and Rudder hope you had fun discovering their ocean home! Crush and Squirt say goodbye too! Remember, beluga whales and sea lions are mammals. This means they breathe air, have warm blood, and have hair. Sea turtles are reptiles. They breathe air too, but their blood is cold.

DORY'S OCEAN HOME

Dory's coral reef is a magical place. It is just one of the habitats in the ocean. Each habitat is part of an ecosystem. The plants and animals in a place help keep it healthy and happy. We are all a part of the amazing balance of life on this planet!

GLOSSARY

adaptation: the way an animal's behavior or part of its body has changed over time so it becomes better fitted to survive

algae: an organism that lives in water that can use the sun's energy to make its food and oxygen. Kelp is a kind of algae.

amphibian: a kind of animal that can live on land and in the water

anglerfish: a fish that lives in the midnight zone. It has a light above its head that it waves around to lure prey.

beluga whale: a small whale that lives in the north and migrates to warm waters every year

blowhole: a hole on top of an ocean mammal's head that it uses for breathing

blubber: a thick layer of fat that keeps whales warm in the cold ocean

blue tang: a saltwater fish that lives in coral reefs and rocky waters close to shore

blue whale: the largest animal on the planet. Blue whales have two blowholes and live worldwide.

camouflage: the way an animal changes color or shape to blend in with its environment

clown fish: a saltwater fish that lives in coral reefs. They make their homes inside of sea anemones. They are one of the few fish that are safe from the anemone's poison.

coastal waters: the part of the ocean closest to land

cold-blooded: an animal whose blood is the same temperature as the air or water around it. Fish and reptiles are cold-blooded.

coral reef: a large colony of coral. A small sea animal related to jellyfish that form a large reef.

cuttlefish: an ocean animal that lives all over the ocean. Cuttlefish are not fish! They are related to octopuses and squid. They are great at camouflage.

dolphin: an ocean mammal that lives worldwide

echinoderm: a family of ocean animals. The family includes the sea star, the sea urchin, and the sea cucumber. Many echinoderms have spiny skin.

echolocation: a way whales use sound to measure the location and shapes of things by using sound waves

ecosystem: a habitat and every living creature within it

fever: a large group of stingrays

filter feeder: an ocean animal that feeds by filtering water. Filter feeders suck in water and filter it past their gills. Then they eat whatever is left. Whale sharks are filter feeders.

fin: a flat part of a fish or ocean mammal that it uses to swim

fish: an animal without legs that lives its whole life in water. Fish are cold-blooded and use gills to breathe oxygen in water.

fluke: the horizontal tail of a whale

food web: a map of all the different plants and animals in one habitat that shows what the plants and animals eat and what eats them

gills: what water-breathing animals use to get oxygen out of water

Great Barrier Reef: the biggest coral reef in the world. The Great Barrier Reef is in Australia. It is 1,600 miles (2,600 km) long.

habitat: the place where an animal or plant lives

intertidal zone: the zone between the tides where the water meets the land in the ocean

kelp: a kind of algae. Kelp is one of the fastest-growing life-forms on the planet.

kelp forest: an ocean habitat made up of large clusters of kelp. Kelp forests are found in colder water.

locomotion: how an animal moves through its environment

loon: a bird that feeds on fish by diving in the water. Loons are excellent underwater swimmers.

mammal: an animal that breathes air. Mammals are warm-blooded and have hair.

midnight zone: the deepest part of the open ocean. Below 3,000 feet (900 m). The midnight zone is freezing cold and pitch-black.

migration: a long journey that an animal makes every year

octopus: a very intelligent, soft-bodied, water-breathing animal that lives in the ocean. Most octopuses live in shallow water. Octopuses have eight legs and three hearts and are mollusks.

open ocean: every part of the ocean that is offshore and not close to land

pod: a group of whales

predator: an animal that eats other animals

ray: a fish related to sharks, with a flattened body and a skeleton made of cartilage. Some rays have a stinging tail and mainly live in warm, shallow water. Many spend most of their time on the ocean floor, but some live in the open ocean.

school: a group of fish

sea anemone: an ocean animal that lives stuck to rocks and coral. Sea anemones have stinging tentacles. They use them to catch prey. Clown fish are immune to their poison.

sea lion: an amphibious mammal that lives in coastal waters. Sea lions have back flippers that they can use to walk on land.

sea otter: an amphibious mammal that lives in coastal waters. Sea otters have thick fur and sleep floating on their backs.

sea star: an ocean animal that lives on the sea floor. Often found in the intertidal zone. Sea stars move very slowly and hold on to the rocks with small suction-cupped tube feet.

sea turtle: an ocean reptile. Sea turtles live worldwide. They lay eggs on beaches and can hold their breath for hours.

sea urchin: an ocean animal related to sea stars that has many spines. Some urchins feed on kelp.

sperm whale: a large toothed whale. Sperm whales have the biggest brains in the world.

sunlight zone: the zone between the ocean surface and 600 feet (180 m) deep. Mammals like whales and sea lions spend most of their lives in the sunlight zone.

surgeonfish: a family of fish that includes the blue tang. They are named surgeonfish because they all have at least one sharp blade—like a surgeon's knife—next to their tail.

twilight zone: a zone between 600 feet (180 m) and 3,000 feet (900 m) deep in the open ocean. It's dark and cold. No plants live in the twilight zone.

warm-blooded: an animal whose blood is always warm even if the air or water around it is cold. Mammals like whales and people are warm-blooded.

whale shark: the biggest fish in the world. Whale sharks live in the warmer oceans of the world.

INDEX

PHOTO CREDITS

All photos are listed by page number from top to bottom.